MY AMAZING BOOK ABOUT ME TREMENDOUS

BY DONALD J. tRUMP

AGE 72

(BELIEVE ME)

My hands are... NOR

STRONG. **Left Hand**

MY HANDS ARE tOO BIG

GOOD SIZE.

I WAS ON LINE SHAKING HANDS WITH SUPPORTERS AND ONE OF THE SUPPORTERS SAID, "MR. tRUMP, YOU HAVE STRONG HANDS, YOU HAVE GOOD SIZE HANDS." AND THEN ANOTHER ONE WOULD SAY, "OH, YOU HAVE GREAT HANDS, MR. tRUMP. I HAD NO IDEA."

MAL HANDS

Right Hand

GREAt.

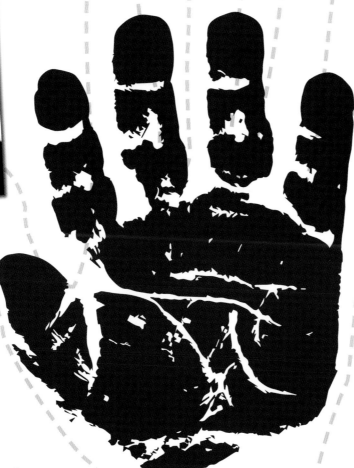

I BUY A SLIGHtLY SMALLER THAN LARGE-SIZE GLOVE, OK?

I HAVE tO SAY tHIS, HE HIt MY HANDS. NOBODY HAS EVER HIt MY HANDS. I'VE NEVER HEARD OF tHIS ONE. LOOK At tHOSE HANDS. ARE tHEY SMALL HANDS?

When I look in the mirror, I see...

I WOULD SAY I SEE A PERSON WHO IS 35 YEARS OLD.

MY FINGERS ARE LONG AND BEAUTIFUL. AS, IT HAS BEEN WELL DOCUMENTED, ARE VARIOUS OTHER PARTS OF MY BODY.

DO I LOOK LIKE A PRESIDENT? HOW HANDSOME AM I, RIGHT? HOW HANDSOME?

I FEEL LIKE A SUPERMODEL EXCEPT, LIKE, TIMES 10, OK? IT'S TRUE. I'M A SUPERMODEL.

$\times 10 =$

HEIDI KLUM.
SADLY, SHE'S NO
LONGER A 10.

My hair is...

SOME REALLY DUMB BLOGGER FOR FAILING
VANITY FAIR, A MAGAZINE WHOSE ADS
ARE DOWN ALMOST 18% THIS YEAR, SAID
I WEAR A HAIRPIECE—I DON'T!

IT IS NOT
A WIG, IT'S
MY HAIR.

Draw
your hair:

I WILL NEVER
CHANGE tHIS HAIRStYLE.
I LIKE It. It FItS MY HEAD.

My hair routine is...

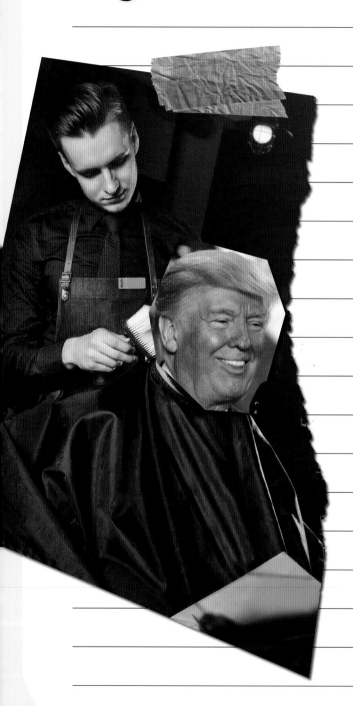

I GET UP, TAKE A SHOWER AND WASH MY HAIR. THEN I READ THE NEWSPAPERS AND WATCH THE NEWS ON TELEVISION, AND SLOWLY THE HAIR DRIES. IT TAKES ABOUT AN HOUR. I DON'T USE A BLOW-DRYER. ONCE IT'S DRY I COMB IT. ONCE I HAVE IT THE WAY I LIKE IT—EVEN THOUGH NOBODY ELSE LIKES IT—I SPRAY IT AND IT'S GOOD FOR THE DAY.

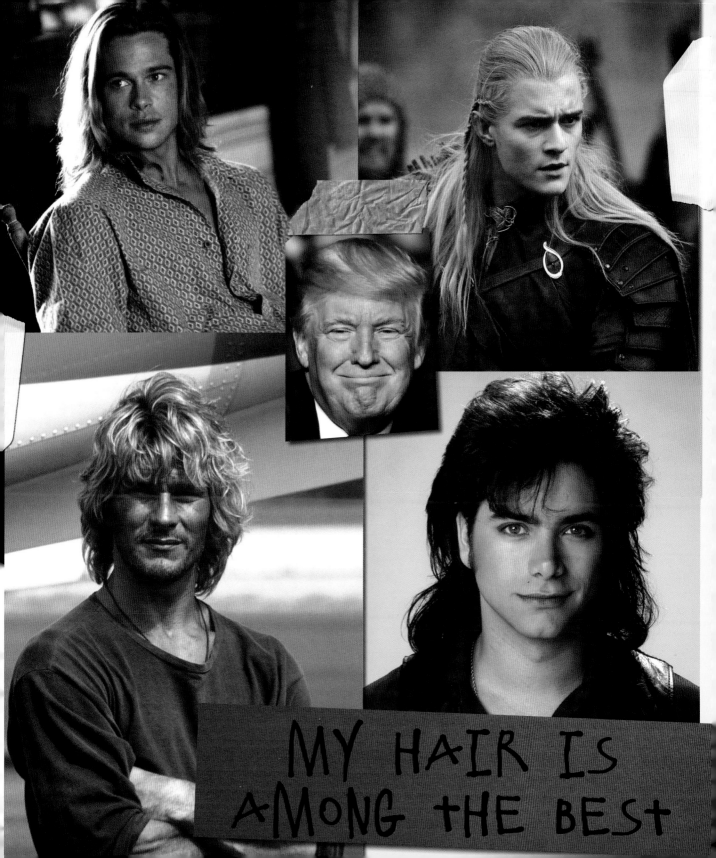

MY HAIR IS AMONG THE BEST

I went to the doctor and...

PEOPLE ARE AMAZED
BECAUSE I DON'T GET MUCH WITH THE COLDS.

healthiest individual ever elected to the presidency

strength and physical stamina are extraordinary

laboratory test results were astonishingly excellent

HAROLD BORNSTEIN

Some people have just great genes. I told the president that if he had a healthier diet over the last 20 years, he might live to be 200 years old.

RONNY JACKSON ADMIRAL DOCTOR IS ONE OF THE FINEST MEN THAT I'VE MET OVER THE LAST LONG PERIOD OF TIME. HIGH QUALITY.

I exercise by...

WHEN I'M SPEAKING IN FRONT OF 15 AND 20,000 PEOPLE AND I'M UP THERE USING A LOT OF MOTION, I GUESS IN ITS OWN WAY, IT'S A PRETTY HEALTHY ACT. I REALLY ENJOY DOING IT. A LOT OF TIMES THESE ROOMS ARE VERY HOT, LIKE SAUNAS, AND I GUESS THAT IS A FORM OF EXERCISE AND, YOU KNOW?

It's OK to be sad. I get sad when...

NEWSWEEK ENDING PRINT EDITION—SAD. NOW MY NEWSWEEK COVERS MEAN NOTHING —THEY LOST ALL CREDIBILITY.

WHILE NOT AT ALL PRESIDENTIAL I MUST POINT OUT THAT THE SLOPPY MICHAEL MOORE SHOW ON BROADWAY WAS A TOTAL BOMB AND WAS FORCED TO CLOSE.

SAD!

SO SAD THAT BURT REYNOLDS HAS LOST ALL OF HIS MONEY. I WISH HE CAME TO ME FOR ADVICE—HE WOULD BE RICH AS HELL!

IT'S VERY SAD THAT REPUBLICANS, EVEN SOME THAT WERE CARRIED OVER THE LINE ON MY BACK, DO VERY LITTLE TO PROTECT THEIR PRESIDENT.

It's even OK to get mad!

It's AMAZING THAT PEOPLE CAN SAY SUCH BAD THINGS ABOUT ME BUT IF I SAY BAD THINGS ABOUT THEM, IT BECOMES A NATIONAL INCIDENT.

HOW COME EVERY TIME I SHOW ANGER, DISGUST OR IMPATIENCE, ENEMIES SAY I HAD A TANTRUM OR MELTDOWN—STUPID OR DISHONEST PEOPLE?

I feel better when I...

IT MAKES ME FEEL SO GOOD TO HIT "SLEAZEBAGS" BACK—MUCH BETTER THAN SEEING A PSYCHIATRIST (WHICH I NEVER HAVE!)

My family is... _____

↑

MELANIA IS A WONDERFUL MOTHER. SHE TAKES CARE OF THE BABY AND I PAY ALL OF THE COSTS.

NOW I KNOW MELANIA, I'M NOT GONNA BE DOING THE DIAPERS, I'M NOT GONNA BE MAKING THE FOOD, I MAY NEVER EVEN SEE THE KIDS.

I'M A REALLY GOOD FATHER, BUT NOT A REALLY GOOD HUSBAND.

FOR A MAN TO BE SUCCESSFUL HE NEEDS SUPPORT AT HOME, JUST LIKE MY FATHER HAD FROM MY MOTHER, NOT SOMEONE WHO IS ALWAYS GRIPING AND BITCHING.

When I was really little...

AS A KID, I WAS MAKING A BUILDING WITH BLOCKS IN OUR PLAYROOM. I DIDN'T HAVE ENOUGH. SO I ASKED MY YOUNGER BROTHER ROBERT IF I COULD BORROW SOME OF HIS. HE SAID, 'OKAY, BUT YOU HAVE TO GIVE THEM BACK WHEN YOU'RE DONE.' I USED ALL OF MY BLOCKS, THEN ALL OF HIS BLOCKS, AND WHEN I WAS DONE I HAD A GREAT BUILDING, WHICH I THEN GLUED TOGETHER. ROBERT NEVER DID GET THOSE BLOCKS BACK.

I'M VERY PROUD 'CAUSE DON AND
ERIC AND IVANKA AND, YOU KNOW,
TO A LESSER EXTENT CAUSE
SHE JUST GOT OUT OF SCHOOL,
OUT OF COLLEGE, BUT, UH, TIFFANY,
WHO'S ALSO BEEN SO TERRIFIC.

THE HARDEST THING FOR ME ABOUT RAISING KIDS HAS BEEN FINDING THE TIME. I KNOW FRIENDS WHO LEAVE THEIR BUSINESS SO THEY CAN SPEND MORE TIME WITH THEIR CHILDREN, AND I SAY, "GIMME A BREAK!" MY CHILDREN COULD NOT LOVE ME MORE IF I SPENT FIFTEEN TIMES MORE TIME WITH THEM.

YOU'VE PROBABLY FIGURED OUT MY CHILDREN REALLY LIKE ME—LOVE ME—A LOT.

I HAVE A SON. HE'S 10 YEARS OLD. HE HAS COMPUTERS. HE IS SO GOOD WITH THESE COMPUTERS. IT'S UNBELIEVABLE.

MY BEAUTIFUL DAUGHTER

My house is...

I ALWAYS HEAR ABOUT THE ELITE...

I LIVE IN A BIGGER MORE BEAUTIFUL APARTMENT AND I LIVE IN THE WHITE HOUSE TOO, WHICH IS REALLY GREAT.

I ALSO WANT TO THANK...EVERYBODY WHO WORKS TO KEEP THIS INCREDIBLE HOUSE, OR BUILDING, OR WHATEVER YOU WANT TO CALL IT — BECAUSE THERE REALLY IS NO NAME FOR IT. IT'S SPECIAL. AND WE KEEP IT IN TIP-TOP SHAPE. WE CALL IT SOMETIMES "TIPPY-TOP SHAPE," AND IT'S A GREAT, GREAT PLACE.

BELIEVE ME, EVERYBODY WANTS TO WORK IN THE WHITE HOUSE. THEY ALL WANT A PIECE OF THAT OVAL OFFICE.

SO MUCH FAKE NEWS ABOUT WHAT IS GOING ON IN THE WHITE HOUSE

These are some of my favorite things...

MANY PEOPLE HAVE COMMENTED tHAT MY FRAGRANCE, "SUCCESS" IS tHE BESt SCENt & LAStS tHE LONGESt.

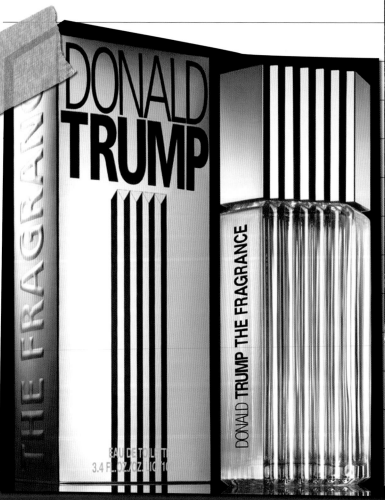

WE'RE GOING TO HAVE ↗
PROFESSORS AND ADJUNCT
PROFESSORS THAT ARE
ABSOLUTELY TERRIFIC.
TERRIFIC PEOPLE, TERRIFIC
BRAINS, SUCCESSFUL. WE
ARE GOING TO HAVE THE
BEST OF THE BEST.

I like to visit...

THE TRUMP BUI[L]

40 WALL STREET ACTUALLY WAS THE SECOND-TALLEST BUILDING IN DOWNTOWN MANHATTAN, AND IT WAS ACTUALLY, BEFORE THE WORLD TRADE CENTER, WAS THE TALLEST—AND THEN, WHEN THEY BUILT THE WORLD TRADE CENTER, IT BECAME KNOWN AS THE SECOND-TALLEST. AND NOW IT'S THE TALLEST.

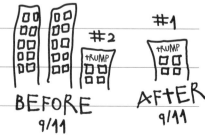

BEFORE 9/11

#2 TRUMP

#1 TRUMP

AFTER 9/11

I OWN A HOUSE IN CHARLOTTESVILLE. DOES ANYONE KNOW I OWN A HOUSE IN CHARLOTTESVILLE? IT'S IN CHARLOTTESVILLE. YOU'LL SEE. IT IS THE WINERY. I MEAN I KNOW A LOT ABOUT CHARLOTTESVILLE. CHARLOTTESVILLE IS A GREAT PLACE THAT'S BEEN VERY BADLY HURT OVER THE LAST COUPLE OF DAYS. I OWN ACTUALLY ONE OF THE LARGEST WINERIES IN THE UNITED STATES. IT'S IN CHARLOTTESVILLE.

YOU ALSO HAD PEOPLE THAT WERE VERY FINE PEOPLE ON BOTH SIDES.

My favorite COMMERCIAL is...

BELIEVE ME,
I UNDERSTAND STEAKS

TRUMP STEAKS: COMMERCIAL SCRIPT

DONALD TRUMP

When it comes to great steaks, I've just raised the stakes. The Sharper Image is one of my favorite stores, with fantastic products of all kinds. That's why I'm thrilled they agree with me: Trump Steaks are the world's greatest steaks, and I mean that in every sense of the word. And The Sharper Image is the only store where you can buy them. Trump Steaks are by far the best tasting, most flavorful beef you've ever had. Truly in a league of their own. Trump Steaks are five-star, gourmet-quality that belong in a very, very select category of restaurant and are certified Angus beef prime. There's nothing better than that. Of all of the beef produced in America, less than 1 percent qualifies for that category. It's the best of the best. Until now you could only enjoy steaks of this quality in one of my resort restaurants or America's finest steakhouses, but now that's changed. Today through The Sharper Image, you can enjoy the world's greatest steaks in your own home, with family, friends, anytime. Trump Steaks are aged to perfection to provide the ultimate in tenderness and flavor. If you like your steak, you'll absolutely love Trump Steaks. Treat yourself to the very, very best life has to offer. And as a gift, Trump Steaks are the best you can give. One bite and you'll know exactly what I'm talking about. And believe me, I understand steaks, it's my favorite food. And these are the best.

People like me because:

Just so you know, I am the least racist person, the least racist person that you've ever seen, the least.

DID YOU KNOW MY NAME IS IN MORE BLACK SONGS THAN ANY OTHER NAME IN HIP-HOP? BLACK ENTERTAINERS LOVE DONALD TRUMP. RUSSELL SIMMONS TOLD ME THAT. RUSSELL SAID, "YOU'RE IN MORE HIP-HOP SONGS THAN ANY OTHER PERSON," LIKE FIVE OF THEM LATELY. THAT'S A GREAT HONOR FOR ME.

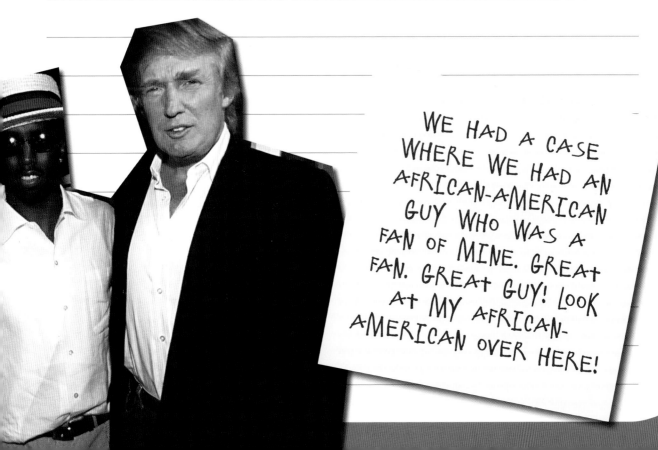

WE HAD A CASE WHERE WE HAD AN AFRICAN-AMERICAN GUY WHO WAS A FAN OF MINE. GREAT FAN. GREAT GUY! LOOK AT MY AFRICAN-AMERICAN OVER HERE!

PEOPLE LOVE ME BECAUSE

I COULD STAND IN THE MIDDLE OF FIFTH AVENUE AND SHOOT SOMEBODY, AND I WOULDN'T LOSE ANY VOTERS, OK? IT'S, LIKE, INCREDIBLE.

I HAVE tREMENDOUS RESPECt FOR WOMEN AND tHE MANY ROLES tHEY SERVE tHAt ARE VItAL to tHE FABRIC OF OUR SOCIEtY AND OUR ECONOMY.

I WOULDN't SAY I'M A FEMINISt. I tHINK tHAt WOULD BE, MAYBE, GOING too FAR.

Five things I'm ~~good~~ BEST at are:

1 I BUILD tHE BESt BUILDINGS, AND I'M tHE BIGGESt DEVELOPER IN NEW YORK BY FAR

OtHER BUILDINGS

MINE

tRUMP

2 PARt OF tHE BEAUtY OF ME IS tHAt I'M VERY RICH.

3 SORRY LOSERS AND HATERS, BUT MY I.Q. IS ONE OF THE HIGHEST—AND YOU ALL KNOW IT! PLEASE DON'T FEEL SO STUPID OR INSECURE. IT'S NOT YOUR FAULT.

4 THERE IS NOBODY WHO UNDERSTANDS THE HORROR OF NUCLEAR MORE THAN ME

5 ONE OF THE GREAT MEMORIES OF ALL TIME.

My ^(FORMER) Best Friends

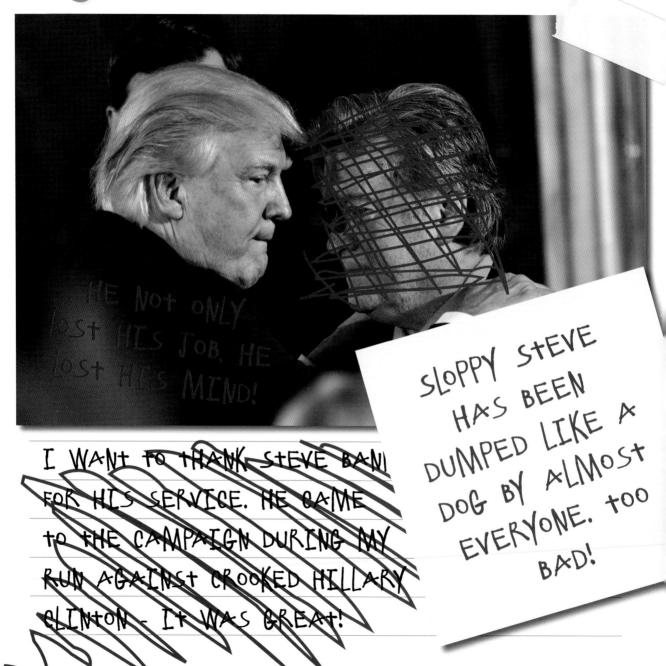

HE NOT ONLY LOST HIS JOB, HE LOST HIS MIND!

I WANT TO THANK STEVE BANN~~ON~~ FOR HIS SERVICE. HE CAME TO THE CAMPAIGN DURING MY RUN AGAINST CROOKED HILLARY CLINTON - IT WAS GREAT!

SLOPPY STEVE HAS BEEN DUMPED LIKE A DOG BY ALMOST EVERYONE. TOO BAD!

JEFF SESSIONS, A
FITTING SELECTION
FOR ATTORNEY
GENERAL

I'M VERY
DISAPPOINTED IN
JEFF SESSIONS.

Someone I really want to meet is...

I THINK I'D GET ALONG VERY WELL WITH
VLADIMIR PUTIN. I JUST THINK SO.
PEOPLE SAY, "WHAT DO YOU MEAN?"
I THINK I WOULD GET ALONG WELL WITH HIM.

I WAS IN RUSSIA. I
WAS IN MOSCOW RECENTLY.
AND I SPOKE INDIRECTLY
—AND DIRECTLY—WITH
PRESIDENT PUTIN. WHO
COULD NOT HAVE BEEN
NICER.

DO YOU THINK PUTIN
WILL BE GOING TO
THE MISS UNIVERSE
PAGEANT IN NOVEMBER
IN MOSCOW—IF SO, WILL
HE BECOME MY NEW
BEST FRIEND?

CALLED ME A GENIUS, I LIKE HIM SO FAR.

My favorite foods are...

YOU CAN tAKE tHE toP OF tHE PIZZA OFF.
YOU'RE NOt JUSt EAtING tHE CRUSt. I LIKE
NOt tO EAt tHE CRUSt SO tHAt
WE KEEP tHE WEIGHt DOWN
At LEASt AS GOOD AS
POSSIBLE.

My favorite McDonald's is...

tHE FISH DELIGHt SOMEtIMES.
tHE BIG MACS ARE GREAt. tHE
QUARtER POUNDERS WItH CHEESE.

My favorite dessert is...

WE HAD tHE MOSt BEAUtIFUL
PIECE OF CHOCOLAtE CAKE
tHAt YOU'VE EVER SEEN. AND
PRESIDENt XI WAS ENJOYING It

Quotes I find interesting...

YOU DON'T HAVE to AGREE WItH tRUMP BUt tHE MOB CAN'T MAKE ME NOt LOVE HIM. WE ARE ßOtH DRAGON ENERGY. HE IS MY BROtHER. I LOVE EVERYONE. I DON'T AGREE WItH EVERYtHING ANYONE DOES. tHAt'S WHAt MAKES US INDIVIDUALS. AND WE HAVE tHE RIGHt to INDEPENDENt tHOUGHt.

—KANYE WESt

tHANK YOU KANYE, VERY cOOL!

MY FAVORItE PARt IS WHEN SAM HAS HIS GUN OUt IN tHE DINER AND HE tELLS tHE GUY to tELL HIS GIRLFRIEND to SHUt UP. "tELL tHAt BItCH to BE COOL. SAY: 'BItCH BE COOL.'" I LOVE tHOSE LINES.

42

BE YARDSTICK OF QUALITY. SOME PEOPLE AREN'T USED TO AN ENVIRONMENT WHERE EXCELLENCE IS EXPECTED.
—STEVE JOBS ↖

I'VE ALWAYS BEEN A FAN OF STEVE JOBS, ESPECIALLY AFTER WATCHING APPLE STOCK COLLAPSE W/OUT HIM — BUT THE YACHT HE BUILT IS TRULY UGLY.

YOU HAVE TO LEARN THE RULES OF THE GAME. AND THEN YOU HAVE TO PLAY BETTER THAN ANYONE ELSE.
—ALBERT EINSTEIN

IT IS BETTER TO LIVE ONE DAY AS A LION THAN 100 YEARS AS A SHEEP.
↗—BENITO MUSSOLINI

IT'S A VERY GOOD QUOTE, IT'S A VERY INTERESTING QUOTE, AND I KNOW IT.

On <u>INAUGURATION DAY</u> I had so much fun!

<u>I LOOKED OUT, THE FIELD WAS, IT LOOKED LIKE A MILLION, MILLION AND A HALF PEOPLE.</u>

I LOOKED OVER tHAt SEA OF PEOPLE, AND I SAID to MYSELF, "WOW," AND I'VE SEEN CROWDS BEFORE. BIG, BIG CROWDS. tHAt WAS SOME CROWD.

photographs of the inaugural proceedings were intentionally framed in a way, in one particular tweet, to minimize the enormous support that had gathered on the National Mall. This was the first time in our nation's history that floor coverings have been used to protect the grass on the Mall. That had the effect of highlighting any areas where people were not standing, while in years past the grass eliminated this visual.

People I Like...

I LIKE MICHAEL DOUGLAS!

tOM IS MY FRIEND AND A tOtAL WINNER

tOM BRADY'S A FRIEND OF MINE. WE PLAY GOLF tOGETHER—THE GREAt QUARtERBACK; HE'S A PHENOMENAL GUY, GREAt AtHLEtE. I'M WITH HIM AND I FEEL THE SAME AGE AS HIM.

← MY NEW FOUND FRIEND JUStIN tRUDEAU!

BILLY JOEL LOVE YOUR MUSIC!

LOVE HISPANICS!

I LIKE MEXICO AND LOVE THE SPIRIT OF MEXICAN PEOPLE, BUT WE MUST PROTECT OUR BORDERS FROM PEOPLE, FROM ALL OVER, POURING INTO THE U.S.

MORE THINGS I LIKE

I LIKE to DRIVE.

I ♥ TRUCKS

I LIKE WINNING!

YOU KNOW, I'VE HAD GREAT SUCCESS. EVEN IN GOLF, I'VE WON MANY GOLF CLUB CHAMPIONSHIPS. I DON'T KNOW IF YOU GUYS PLAY GOLF. BUT TO WIN A CLUB CHAMPIONSHIP IS HARD, LITERALLY HARD. AND YOU HAVE TO BEAT SCRATCH PLAYERS. YOU GOT A LOT OF GOOD PLAYERS.

MY LIFE HAS BEEN ABOUT WINNING. MY LIFE HAS NOT BEEN ABOUT LOSING.

EVEN MORE tHINGS I LIKE

YOU KNOW, It REALLY DOESN't MATTER WHAT tHEY WRITE AS LONG AS YOU'VE GOt A YOUNG AND BEAUTIFUL PIECE OF ASS.

OFTENTIMES WHEN I WAS SLEEPING WITH ONE OF THE TOP WOMEN IN THE WORLD I WOULD SAY TO MYSELF, THINKING ABOUT ME AS A BOY FROM QUEENS, "CAN YOU BELIEVE WHAT I AM GETTING?"

I'M AUTOMATICALLY ATTRACTED TO BEAUTIFUL—I JUST START KISSING THEM.

Things I Like on TV...

MY GUILtY-PLEASURE tV SHOW—"SNL." StARRING ME. tHEY GOt GREAt RAtINGS. tHE BESt RAtINGS IN YEARS. It WAS A tERRIFIC SUCCESS. I ENJOYED DOING It. It WAS 50 PERCENt MORE tHAN HILLARY'S SHOW. tHAt MAKES ME FEEL GOOD.

THE MOST INFLUENTIAL SHOW IN NEWS

FOX & FRIENDS

THREE GREAT PEOPLE!
THE MANY FAKE NEWS HATE
SHOWS SHOULD STUDY YOUR
FORMULA FOR SUCCESS!

Leaders I Look Up To...

HE'S A FANTASTIC GUY....HE tooK CONTROL OF EGYPT. AND HE REALLY tooK CONTROL OF It.

ABDEL
FATTAH
EL SISI

LOVE YOUR
SHOES.
BOY, tHOSE
SHOES.
MAN...

WE'VE HAD A GREAT RELATIONSHIP.

RODRIGO DUTERTE

I JUST WANTED to CONGRATULATE YOU BECAUSE I AM HEARING OF THE UNBELIEVABLE JOB ON THE DRUG PROBLEM.

RECEP TAYYIP ERDOGAN

HE'S BECOME A FRIEND OF MINE. WE HAVE A GREAT FRIENDSHIP AS COUNTRIES. I THINK WE'RE, RIGHT NOW, AS CLOSE AS WE HAVE EVER BEEN. AND A LOT OF THAT HAS TO DO WITH THE PERSONAL RELATIONSHIP.

I AM A DEFENDER OF MILEY CYRUS, WHO I THINK IS A GOOD PERSON (AND NOT BECAUSE SHE STAYS AT MY HOTELS)

EVEN MORE (MORE) PEOPLE I LIKE

I THINK EMINEM IS FANTASTIC, AND MOST PEOPLE THINK I WOULDN'T LIKE EMINEM.

THE NEW POPE IS A HUMBLE MAN, VERY MUCH LIKE ME, WHICH PROBABLY EXPLAINS WHY I LIKE HIM SO MUCH!

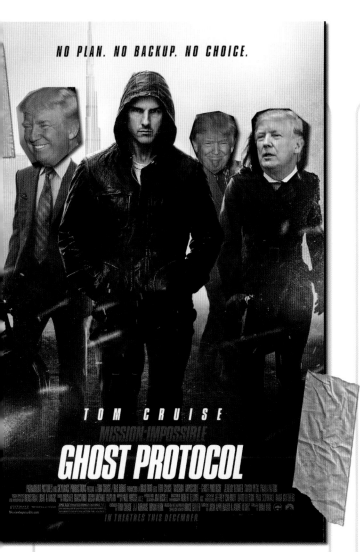

NO PLAN. NO BACKUP. NO CHOICE.

TOM CRUISE

MISSION: IMPOSSIBLE
GHOST PROTOCOL

IN THEATRES THIS DECEMBER

I DON'T CARE WHAT PEOPLE SAY. I LIKE tOM CRUISE. HE WORKS HIS ASS OFF AND NEVER EVER QUItS. HE'S ONE OF THE FEW tRUE MOVIE StARS.

ROSIE IS CRUDE, RUDE, OBNOXIOUS AND DUMB —OtHER THAN tHAt I LIKE HER VERY MUCH!

EVERYONE KNOWS I AM RIGHt tHAt ROBERt PAttINSON SHOULD DUMP KRIStEN StEWARt. IN A COUPLE OF YEARS, HE WILL tHANK ME. BE SMARt, ROBERt.

FOX NEWS MItt ROMNEY DAVID BROOKS

Things, People and Places I Don't Like...

STEVE BANNON

MEXICO

THE WASHINGTON POST

MEGYN KELLY   COLIN KAEPERNICK

ABC NEWS   MACY'S BRITAIN CBS

JOE BIDEN

LAVAR BALL

FAKE NEWS

RUTH BADER GINSBURG   GLENN BECK

THE ASSOCIATED PRESS   JOY BEHAR

ROSIE O'DONNELL   MICHAEL BLOOMBERG

DEMOCRATS MItCH MCCONNELL

CHELSEA MANNING

RONDA ROUSEY   MAJOR LEAGUE BASEBALL   MAUREEN DOWD

SATURDAY NIGHt LIVE

U.S. POSTAL SERVICE   CORY BOOKER   U.S. CONGRESS

JOHN MCCAIN   CHRIS CHRISTIE   COLIN POWELL

AMAZON

HUMA ABEDIN   MIKA BRZEZINSKI POLItICO

WHOOPI GOLDBERG   LINDSEY GRAHAM

CENTRAL PARK FIVE

CROOKED

GEORGE BUSH F.B.I. ESPN

GEORGE W. BUSH THE VIEW

JEB BUSH PAUL RYAN CARLY

HILLARY FIORINA

JEFF CHINA ANGELA
FLAKE MERKEL

FIRE AND FURY:
INSIDE THE TRUMP THE ELECTORAL PROCESS
WHITE HOUSE

MEET THE PRESS SAUDI ARABIA MERYL
STREEP

BARACK OBAMA

THE WALL STREET JOURNAL USA TODAY

UCLA BASKETBALL PLAYERS UNIVISION

BEN CARSON THE FAILING
ALICIA MACHADO

RAND PAUL NEW YORK TIMES

BILL CLINTON CRYIN CHUCK SCHUMER

GEORGE PATAKI MARSHAWN LYNCH

JOE SCARBOROUGH ELIZABETH

J.S. LEGAL NANCY WARREN
SYSTEM PELOSI

VANITY FAIR MAGAZINE RICK PERRY

KATHY GRIFFIN DOUG JONES

KRISTEN STEWART

59

My penpal is...
LIttLE ROCKEt MAN

WHY WOULD KIM JONG-UN INSULt ME BY CALLING ME "OLD," WHEN I WOULD NEVER CALL HIM "SHORt AND FAt?" OH WELL. I tRY SO HARD tO BE HIS FRIEND—AND MAYBE SOMEDAY tHAt WILL HAPPEN!

HIS BUttON

MY BUttON

My catchphrase is...

THE LINE OF 'MAKE AMERICA GREAT AGAIN.' THE PHRASE, THAT WAS MINE. I CAME UP WITH IT ABOUT A YEAR AGO, AND I KEPT USING IT, AND EVERYBODY'S USING IT, THEY ARE ALL LOVING IT. I DON'T KNOW, I GUESS I SHOULD COPYRIGHT IT, MAYBE I HAVE COPYRIGHTED IT.

TRUMP
~~REAGAN~~

FOR PRESIDENT
Let's make America great again.

TRUMP
~~REAGAN~~ in '80

Make America Great Again

What I've learned from my mistakes...

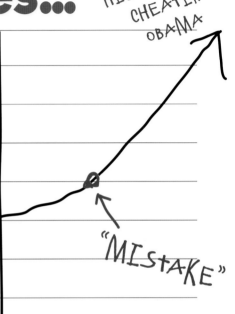

HIGHER THAN CHEATIN' OBAMA

I DON'T tHINK I'VE MADE MISTAKES. EVERY tIME SOMEBODY SAID I MADE A MISTAKE, tHEY DO tHE POLLS AND MY NUMBERS GO UP, SO I GUESS I HAVEN'T MADE ANY MISTAKES.

tRUMP POLLS

"MISTAKE"

tIME

My favorite weather is...

It's FREEZING AND
SNOWING IN NEW YORK—
WE NEED GLObAL WARMING!

I KNOW MUCH AbOUt CLIMAtE CHANGE. I'D bE — RECEIVED ENVIRONMENtAL

AWARDS. AND I OFtEN JOKE thAt thIS IS DONE FOR thE bENEFIt OF

CHINA. ObVIOUSLY, I JOKE. bUt thIS IS DONE FOR thE bENEFIt OF CHINA,

bECAUSE CHINA DOES NOt ANYthING tO HELP CLIMAtE CHANGE.

YOU CAN'T USE HAIR SPRAY BECAUSE HAIR SPRAY IS GOING TO AFFECT THE OZONE. I'M TRYING TO FIGURE OUT. LET'S SEE, I'M IN MY ROOM IN NEW YORK CITY AND I WANT TO PUT A LITTLE SPRAY SO THAT I CAN—RIGHT? RIGHT? BUT I HEAR WHERE THEY DON'T WANT ME TO USE HAIR SPRAY, THEY WANT ME TO USE THE PUMP BECAUSE THE OTHER ONE WHICH I REALLY LIKE BETTER THAN GOING BING, BING, BING—AND THEN IT COMES OUT IN BIG GLOBS, RIGHT, AND YOU—IT'S STUCK IN YOUR HAIR AND YOU SAY "OH MY GOD, I'VE GOT TO TAKE A SHOWER AGAIN. MY HAIR'S ALL SCREWED UP." RIGHT? I WANT TO USE HAIR SPRAY. THEY SAY "DON'T USE HAIR SPRAY, IT'S BAD FOR THE OZONE." SO I'M SITTING IN THIS CONCEALED APARTMENT, THIS CONCEALED UNIT—YOU KNOW, I REALLY DO LIVE IN A VERY NICE APARTMENT, RIGHT? BUT IT'S SEALED, IT'S BEAUTIFUL. I DON'T THINK ANYTHING GETS OUT. AND I'M NOT SUPPOSED TO BE USING HAIR SPRAY.

Draw your favorite weather

I'm proud of...

PEOPLE ARE PROUD to BE SAYING MERRY CHRISTMAS AGAIN. I AM PROUD to HAVE LED tHE CHARGE AGAINSt tHE ASSAULt OF OUR CHERISHED AND BEAUtIFUL PHRASE. MERRY CHRIStMAS!!!!!

PEOPLE SHOULD BE PROUD OF tHE FACt tHAt I Got OBAMA to RELEASE HIS BIRtH CERtIFICAtE, WHICH IN A RECENt BOOK HE "MIRACULOUSLY" FOUND.

BE SURE to WATCH "tHE HISTORY OF WRESTLEMANIA" ON NETFLIX. MY INTERVIEW EXPLAINS HOW I SUPPORTED tHE EVENT EARLY ON. I'M PROUD OF It.

I tHINK VIAGRA IS WONDERFUL IF YOU NEED It, IF YOU HAVE MEDICAL ISSUES, IF YOU'VE HAD SURGERY. I'VE JUSt NEVER NEEDED It. FRANKLY, I WOULDN't MIND IF tHERE WERE AN ANtI-VIAGRA, SOMEtHING WItH tHE OPPOSItE EFFECt. I'M NOt BRAGGING. I'M JUSt LUCKY. I DON't NEED It.

My five best ideas are...

1 WE SHOULD HAVE A CONTEST AS TO WHICH OF THE NETWORKS, PLUS CNN AND NOT INCLUDING FOX, IS THE MOST DISHONEST, CORRUPT AND/OR DISTORTED IN ITS POLITICAL COVERAGE OF YOUR FAVORITE PRESIDENT (ME). THEY ARE ALL BAD. WINNER TO RECEIVE THE FAKE NEWS TROPHY!

2 I HAD AN IDEA RECENTLY. WHEN THEY SEND ILLEGALS INTO OUR COUNTRY, WE CHARGE MEXICO $100,000 FOR EVERY ILLEGAL THAT CROSSES THAT BORDER BECAUSE IT'S TROUBLE.

3   I NEVER SAID "GIVE tEACHERS GUNS" ... WHAt I SAID WAS to lOOK At tHE POSSIBILItY OF GIVING "CONCEALED GUNS to GUN ADEPt tEACHERS WItH MILItARY OR SPECIAL tRAINING EXPERIENCE—ONLY tHE BESt. 20% OF tEACHERS,

4 A lOt, WOULD NOW BE ABLE to IMMEDIAtELY FIRE BACK IF A SAVAGE SICKo CAME to A SCHOOL WItH BAD INtENtIONS. AttACKS WOULD END!

5

SPACE IS A WAR-FIGHtING DOMAIN, JUSt LIKE tHE LAND, AIR AND SEA. WE MAY EVEN HAVE A SPACE FORCE.

I'm <u>TOUGH</u> because...

I REALLY BELIEVE I'D RUN IN THERE EVEN IF I DIDN'T HAVE A WEAPON.

CRAZY JOE BIDEN IS TRYING TO ACT LIKE A TOUGH GUY.

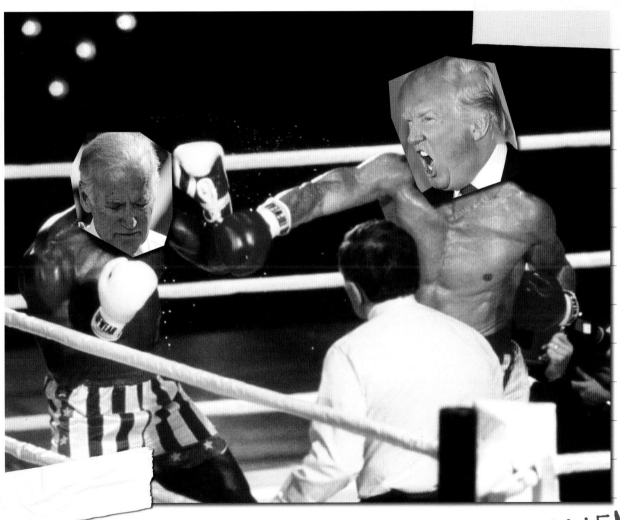

DON'T THREATEN PEOPLE JOE!

If I could talk with someone from the past, it would be...

PRESIDENt ANDREW JACKSON, WHO DIED 16 YEARS BEFORE tHE CIVIL WAR STARtED, SAW It COMING AND WAS ANGRY. WOULD NEVER HAVE LEt It HAPPEN!

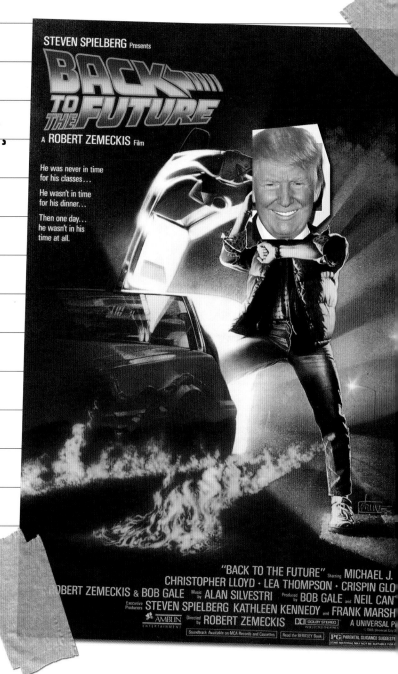

STEVEN SPIELBERG Presents

BACK TO THE FUTURE

A ROBERT ZEMECKIS Film

He was never in time for his classes...

He wasn't in time for his dinner...

Then one day... he wasn't in his time at all.

"BACK TO THE FUTURE" Starring MICHAEL J.
CHRISTOPHER LLOYD · LEA THOMPSON · CRISPIN GLO
OBERT ZEMECKIS & BOB GALE Music by ALAN SILVESTRI Produced by BOB GALE and NEIL CANT
Executive Producers STEVEN SPIELBERG KATHLEEN KENNEDY and FRANK MARSH
AMBLIN ENTERTAINMENT Directed by ROBERT ZEMECKIS DOLBY STEREO IN SELECTED THEATRES A UNIVERSAL P

Soundtrack Available on MCA Records and Cassettes · Read the BERKLEY Book · PG PARENTAL GUIDANCE SUGGESTED

I get the best advice from...

MY PRIMARY CONSULTANT IS **MYSELF.**

I'M SPEAKING WITH MYSELF, NUMBER ONE, BECAUSE I HAVE A VERY GOOD BRAIN. AND I'VE SAID A LOT OF THINGS.

When I grow up, I'm going to be a great PRESIDENT because...

MY ENTIRE LIFE, I'VE WATCHED POLITICIANS BRAGGING ABOUT HOW POOR THEY ARE, HOW THEY CAME FROM NOTHING, HOW POOR THEIR PARENTS AND GRANDPARENTS WERE. AND I SAID TO MYSELF, "IF THEY CAN STAY SO POOR FOR SO MANY GENERATIONS, MAYBE THIS ISN'T THE KIND OF PERSON WE WANT TO BE ELECTING TO HIGHER OFFICE." HOW SMART CAN THEY BE? THEY'RE MORONS.

I WILL BE THE GREATEST JOBS PRESIDENT THAT GOD EVER CREATED.

I WILL
BUILD A
GREAT WALL,
AND NOBODY
BUILDS WALLS
BETTER THAN
ME, BELIEVE
ME, AND
I'LL BUILD
THEM VERY
INEXPENSIVELY. I
WILL BUILD A GREAT, GREAT
WALL ON OUR SOUTHERN BORDER, AND
I WILL MAKE MEXICO PAY FOR
THAT WALL. MARK MY WORDS.

I'VE HAD A BEAUTIFUL, I'VE
HAD A FLAWLESS CAMPAIGN.
YOU'LL BE WRITING BOOKS
ABOUT THIS CAMPAIGN.

I LOVE WOMEN

FIRST OF ALL, NOBODY RESPECTS WOMEN MORE THAN DONALD TRUMP, I'LL TELL YOU. NOBODY RESPECTS WOMEN MORE. MY DAUGHTER IVANKA ALWAYS SAYS, "DADDY, NOBODY RESPECTS WOMEN MORE THAN YOU, DADDY, WHAT ARE THEY TALKING ABOUT?"

I THINK THE ONLY DIFFERENCE BETWEEN ME AND THE OTHER CANDIDATES IS THAT I'M MORE HONEST, AND MY WOMEN ARE MORE BEAUTIFUL.

I CHERISH WOMEN. I WANT TO HELP WOMEN. I'M GOING TO BE ABLE TO DO THINGS FOR WOMEN THAT NO OTHER CANDIDATE WOULD BE ABLE TO DO.

I know all about...

I KNOW MORE ABOUT **ISIS** THAN THE GENERALS DO, BELIEVE ME.
I WOULD BOMB THE SHIT OUT OF THEM.
I WOULD JUST BOMB THOSE SUCKERS.
AND, THAT'S RIGHT, I'D BLOW UP THE PIPES. I'D BLOW UP THE REFINERIES.
I'D BLOW UP EVERY SINGLE INCH.
THERE WOULD BE NOTHING LEFT.

I KNOW OUR **COMPLEX tAX LAWS** BETTER THAN ANYONE WHO HAS EVER RUN FOR PRESIDENT AND AM THE ONLY ONE WHO CAN FIX THEM.

THE ONLY ONE to FIX THE **INFRASTRUCTURE** OF OUR COUNTRY IS ME — ROADS, AIRPORTS, BRIDGES. I KNOW HOW to BUILD, POLS ONLY KNOW HOW to tALK!

I AM GOING to SAVE **SOCIAL SECURItY** WIthOUt ANY CUtS. I KNOW WHERE to GEt THE MONEY FROM. NOBODY ELSE DOES.

I KNOW SOME OF YOU MAY tHINK I'M tOUGH AND HARSH BUt ACTUALLY I'M A VERY COMPASSIONATE PERSON (WITH A VERY HIGH IQ) WITH STRONG COMMON SENSE

79

WHY I AM tHE BESt PRESIDENt

I WAS SUCCESSFUL, SUCCESSFUL, SUCCESSFUL. I WAS ALWAYS tHE BESt AtHLEtE, PEOPLE DON't KNOW tHAt. BUt I WAS SUCCESSFUL At EVERYtHING I EVER DID AND tHEN I RUN FOR PRESIDENt. FIRSt tIME-FIRSt tIME, NOt tHREE tIMES, NOt SIX tIMES. I RAN FOR PRESIDENt FIRSt tIME AND LO AND BEHOLD, I WIN. AND tHEN PEOPLE SAY OH, IS HE A SMARt PERSON? I'M SMARtER tHAN ALL OF tHEM PUt tOGEtHER, BUt tHEY CAN't ADMIt It.

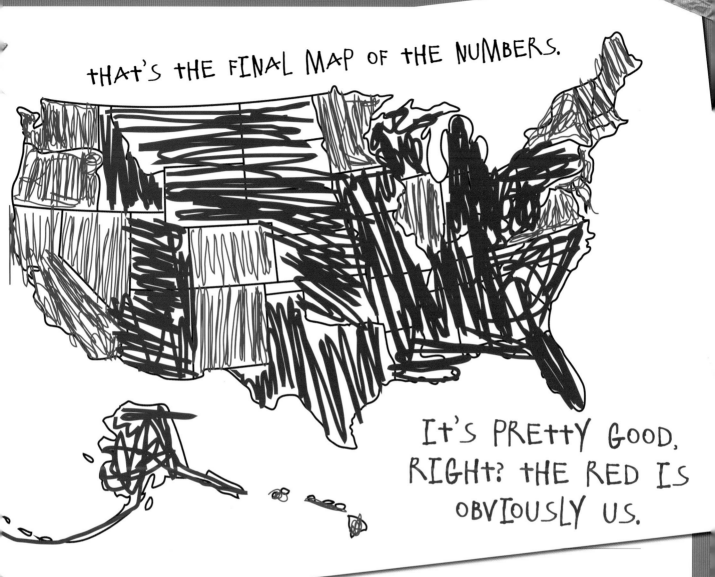

THAT'S THE FINAL MAP OF THE NUMBERS.

IT'S PRETTY GOOD, RIGHT? THE RED IS OBVIOUSLY US.

JUST HAD A VERY OPEN AND SUCCESSFUL PRESIDENTIAL ELECTION. NOW PROFESSIONAL PROTESTERS, INCITED BY THE MEDIA, ARE PROTESTING. VERY UNFAIR!

WHY I AM tHE BESt PRESIDENt

1. I'M A PERSON tHAt WANtS to tELL tHE tRUtH. I'M AN HONESt PERSON, AND WHAt I'M SAYING, YOU KNOW IS EXACtLY RIGHt.

VERY UNFAIR

A BAD JOKE! (tHE $20 BILLION DOLLAR WALL IS "PEANUtS" COMPARED to WHAt MEXICO MAKES FROM tHE U.S. NAFtA IS A BAD JOKE!)

WE LOOK LIKE WE'RE BEGGARS.

→ PARIS CLIMAtE AGREEMENt

NAFtA

↑ WORSt DEAL IN U.S. HISTORY

IRAN NUKE DEAL

HORRIBLE, ONE-SIDED DEAL (tHE FACt IS, tHIS WAS A HORRIBLE ONE-SIDED DEAL tHAt SHOULD HAVE NEVER, EVE BEEN MADE.)

2. I MAKE GOOD DEALS. I DON't MAKE BAD DEALS. I MAKE GOOD DEALS.

I DEAL WITH FOREIGN COUNTRIES, AND DESPITE WHAT YOU MAY READ, I HAVE UNBELIEVABLE RELATIONSHIPS WITH ALL OF THE FOREIGN LEADERS. THEY LIKE ME. I LIKE THEM. YOU KNOW, IT'S AMAZING.

3.

4. I DON'T BELIEVE THAT ANY PRESIDENT HAS ACCOMPLISHED AS MUCH AS THIS PRESIDENT IN THE FIRST SIX OR SEVEN MONTHS. I REALLY DON'T BELIEVE IT.

TRUMP IS HITTING ON ALL FRONTS... EVEN TV!

TIME

Obama's Next Move:
Can He Curb
Health-Care Costs?

How Stressed
Is Your Bank?
A Checkup

DONALD
TRUMP

Global Warming:
A New Age
of Extinction

The "Apprentice"
is a television smash!

TIME MAGAZINE
CALLED TO SAY THAT I
WAS PROBABLY GOING
TO BE NAMED "MAN
(PERSON) OF THE YEAR,"
LIKE LAST YEAR, BUT I
WOULD HAVE TO AGREE
TO AN INTERVIEW AND
A MAJOR PHOTO SHOOT.
I SAID PROBABLY IS NO
GOOD AND TOOK A PASS.
THANKS ANYWAY!

WHY I AM tHE BESt PRESIDENt

MY USE OF SOCIAL MEDIA IS NOt PRESIDENtIAL — It's MODERN DAY PRESIDENtIAL.

MAKE AMERICA GREAt AGAIN!

PRESIDENt

tRUMP

WITH THE EXCEPTION OF THE LATE, GREAT ABRAHAM LINCOLN, I CAN BE MORE PRESIDENTIAL THAN ANY PRESIDENT THAT'S EVER HELD THIS OFFICE.

MOST PEOPLE DON'T EVEN KNOW HE WAS A REPUBLICAN. RIGHT? DOES ANYONE KNOW? A LOT OF PEOPLE DON'T KNOW THAT. WE HAVE TO BUILD THAT UP A LITTLE MORE.

WHY I AM tHE BESt PRESIDENt

tHROUGHOUt MY LIFE, MY tWO GREATESt ASSEtS HAVE BEEN MENtAL StABILItY AND BEING, LIKE, REALLY SMARt I WENt FROM VERY SUCCESSFUL BUSINESSMAN, tO tOP t.V. StAR ... tO PRESIDENt OF tHE UNItED StAtES (ON MY FIRSt tRY). I tHINK tHAt WOULD QUALIFY AS NOt SMARt, BUt GENIUS... AND A <u>VERY StABLE GENIUS</u> At tHAt!

I'M A VERY COMPASSIONAtE PERSON (WItH A VERY HIGH IQ) WItH StRONG COMMON SENSE

WHY I AM the BESt PRESIDENt

I AM ACCOMPLISHING A Lot IN WASHINGtoN!

SINCE tAKING OFFICE I HAVE BEEN VERY StRICt ON COMMERCIAL AVIAtION. GOOD NEWS - It WAS JUSt REPORtED tHAt tHERE WERE ZERO DEAtHS IN 2017, tHE BESt AND SAFESt YEAR ON RECORD!

tHE StOCK MARKEt IS SEttING RECORD AFtER RECORD AND UNEMPLOYMENt IS At A 17 YEAR LOW. SO MANY tHINGS ACCOMPLISHED BY tHE tRUMP ADMINIStRAtION, PERHAPS MORE tHAN ANY OtHER PRESIDENt IN FIRSt YEAR. SADLY, WILL NEVER BE REPORtED CORRECtLY BY tHE FAKE NEWS MEDIA!

ANY NEGATIVE POLLS
ARE FAKE NEWS,
JUST LIKE THE CNN,
ABC, NBC POLLS IN
THE ELECTION.

I GUARANTEE YOU
THERE'S NO PROBLEM.
I GUARANTEE.

It IS VERY
HARD...to
ATTACK ME ON
LOOKS BECAUSE
I AM SO GOOD
LOOKING.

DOING A GREAT JOB

IVANKA tRUMP

JARED KUSHNER

KELLYANNE CONWAY

StEPHEN MILLER

~~STEVE BANNON~~

~~MIKE FLYNN~~

~~REINCE PRIEBUS~~

SEAN SPICER

~~JOHN McENTEE~~

~~GARY COHN~~

~~TOM BOSSERt~~

~~TOM PRICE~~

~~OMAROSA MANIGAULT~~

~~H.R. McMASTER~~

~~ANDREW McCABE~~

HOPE ~~HICKS~~

~~ROB PORTER~~

~~SEBASTIAN GORKA~~

~~REX TILLERSON~~

~~MICHAEL DUBKE~~

~~DR. BRENDA FITZGERALD~~

~~ANTHONY SCARAMUCCI~~

SARAH HUCKABEE SANDERS

THE BESt LAWYERS

RUDY GIULIANI

JAY SEKULOW

~~TY COBB~~

~~ANDREW COHEN~~

~~MARK CORALLO~~

~~MARC KASOWITZ~~

~~JOHN DOWD~~

~~JOSEPH DIGENOVA~~

~~VICTORIA TOENSING~~

EVERYBODY WANtS
tO WORK IN tHE
WHItE HOUSE

CITATIONS Every word in this book, except for the prompts, was spoken, written, tweeted or retweeted by Donald J. Trump either before or during his presidency. Find the source and any necessary context for each quote below. Spelling errors and grammatical mistakes remain unchanged because, well, he's the president. Who are we to judge?

WHEN I LOOK IN THE MIRROR, I SEE...
"I would say I see a person that's 35 years old." *(Dr. Oz interview, 9/15/16)*

"My fingers are long and beautiful, as, it has been well documented, are various other parts of my body." *(To the* New York Post*'s Page Six, 2011)*

"Do I look a president? How handsome am I, right? How handsome?" *(Rally in West Chester, Pennsylvania, 4/25/16)*

"I feel like a supermodel except, like, times 10, OK? It's true. I'm a supermodel." *(Rally in Phoenix, Arizona, 6/18/16)*

"Heidi Klum. Sadly, she's no longer a 10." *(*The New York Times*, 8/15/15)*

MY HANDS ARE...
"Strong." "Good size." "Great."

"My hands are normal hands. I was on line shaking hands with supporters and one of the supporters said, 'Mr. Trump, you have strong hands, you have good size hands.' And then another one would say, 'Oh, you have great hands, Mr. Trump. I had no idea.'"

"My hands are normal. Slightly large, actually. In fact, I buy a slightly smaller than large-size glove, okay? But I did this because everybody was saying to me, 'Oh, your hands are very nice, they're normal.'" *(*The Washington Post*, 3/21/16)*

"I have to say this, he hit my hands. Nobody has ever hit my hands. I've never heard of this one. Look at those hands. Are they small hands?" *(Republican Debate, 3/3/16)*

"My hands are too big." *(Handing out meals at a relief center for flood victims in Houston, 9/2/17)*

MY HAIR IS...
"Some really dumb blogger for failing @VanityFair, a magazine whose ads are down almost 18% this year, said I wear a hairpiece --- I DON'T!" *(Twitter, 7/19/12)*

"I will never change this hairstyle, I like it. It fits my head. Those who criticize me are only losers and envy people. And it is not a wig, it's my hair. Do you want to touch it?" *(Veja, 2014)*

MY HAIR ROUTINE IS...
"I get up, take a shower and wash my hair. Then I read the newspapers and watch the news on television, and slowly the hair dries. It takes about an hour. I don't use a blow-dryer. Once it's dry I comb it. Once I have it the way I like it—even though nobody else likes it—I spray it and it's good for the day." *(Playboy, 2004)*

I WENT TO THE DOCTOR AND...
"...people are amazed because I don't get much with the colds." *(Dr. Oz interview, 9/15/16)*

"healthiest individual ever elected to the presidency," "strength and physical stamina are extraordinary," "laboratory test results were astonishingly excellent," *(Letter from Dr. Harold M. Bornstein, 12/4/15. On 5/1/18, Bornstein alleged that Trump dictated the letter.)*

"Some people have just great genes. I told the president that if he had a healthier diet over the last 20 years, he might live to be 200 years old." *(Press conference given by White House physician Dr. Ronny Jackson, 1/16/18)*

"Ronny Jackson—admiral, doctor—is one of the finest men that I've met over the last long period of time. High quality." *(White House press conference, 4/27/18)*

I EXERCISE BY...
"When I'm speaking in front of 15 and 20,000 people and I'm up there using a lot of motion, I guess in it's own way, it's a pretty healthy act. I really enjoy doing it. A lot of times these rooms are very hot, like saunas, and I guess that is a form of exercise and, you know?" *(Dr. Oz interview, 9/15/16)*

IT'S OK TO BE SAD. I GET SAD WHEN...
"Newsweek ending print edition--sad. Now my Newsweek covers mean nothing--they lost all credibility. TIME to follow?" *(Twitter, 10/18/12)*

"While not at all presidential I must point out that the Sloppy Michael Moore Show on Broadway was a TOTAL BOMB and was forced to close. Sad!" *(Twitter, 10/28/17)*

"So sad that Burt Reynolds has lost all of his money. I wish he came to me for advice--he would be rich as hell!" *(Twitter, 12/2/14)*

"It's very sad that Republicans, even some that were carried over the line on my back, do very little to protect their President." *(Twitter, 7/23/17)*

IT'S EVEN OK TO GET MAD!
"It's amazing that people can say such bad things about me but if I say bad things about them, it becomes a national incident." *(Twitter, 1/9/13)*

"How come every time I show anger, disgust or impatience, enemies say I had a tantrum or meltdown—stupid or dishonest people?" *(Twitter, 11/12/12)*

I FEEL BETTER WHEN I...
"It makes me feel so good to hit 'sleazebags' back -- much better than seeing a psychiatrist (which I never have!)" *(Twitter, 11/19/12)*

MY FAMILY IS...
"Melania is a wonderful mother. She takes care of the baby and I pay all of the costs." *(Interview with Howard Stern, 2005)*

"Now I know Melania, I'm not gonna to be doing the diapers, I'm not gonna be making the food, I may never even see the kids." *(Interview with CNN's Larry King, 5/17/05)*

"I'm a really good father, but not a really good husband. You've probably figured out my children really like me—love me—a lot. It's hard when somebody walks into the living room of Mar-a-Lago in Palm Beach and this is supposed to be, like, a normal life. But they're very grounded and very solid. The hardest thing for me about raising kids has been finding the time. I know friends who leave their business so they can spend more time with their children, and I say, 'Gimme a break!' My children could not love me more if I spent fifteen times more time with them." *(*New York Magazine*, 2004)*

"For a man to be successful he needs support at home, just like my father had from my mother, not someone who is always griping and bitching." *(*The Art of the Comeback*, 1997)*

"I'm very proud 'cause Don and Eric and Ivanka and, you know, to a lesser extent cause she just got out of school, out of college, but, uh, Tiffany, who's also been so terrific." *(*Fox & Friends*, 11/8/16)*

"I have a son. He's 10 years old. He has computers. He is so good with these computers, it's unbelievable." *(First Presidential Debate, 9/26/16)*

"As a kid, I was making a building with blocks in our playroom. I didn't have enough. So I asked my younger brother Robert if I could borrow some of his. He said, 'Okay, but you have to give them back when you're done.' I used all of my blocks, then all of his blocks, and when I was done I had a great building, which I then glued together. Robert never did get those blocks back." *(*Esquire*, J 2004)*

MY BEAUTIFUL DAUGHTER
"My daughter, Ivanka. She's 6 feet tall, she's got the best body." *(*The Howard Stern Show*, 2003)*

"Yeah, she's really something, and what a beauty, that one. If I weren't happily married and, ya know, her father..." *(*Rolling Stone*, 2015)*

"I don't think Ivanka would do that inside the magazine. Although she does have a very nice figure. I've said that if Ivanka weren't my daughter, perhaps I would be dating her." *(*The View*, 2006)*

MY HOUSE IS...
"Now, you know, I was a good student. I always hear about the elite. You know, the elite. They're elite? I went to better schools than they did. I was a better student than they were. I live in a bigger, more beautiful apartment, and I live in the White House, too, which is really great." *(Rally in Phoenix, Arizona, 8/22/17)*

"I also want to thank the White House Historical Association, [...] and everybody who works to keep this incredible house, or building, or whatever you want to call it—because there really is no name for it. It's special. And we keep it in tip-top shape. We call it sometimes 'tippy-top shape,' and it's a great, great place." *(White House Easter Egg Roll, 2018)*

"Believe me, everybody wants to work in the White House. They all want a piece of that Oval Office." *(White House press conference, 3/6/18)*

"So much Fake News about what is going on in the White House." *(Twitter, 4/11/18)*

MY OTHER HOUSE IS...
"Gliding through his gilded home, he bragged that people have called his Manhattan aerie the 'best apartment ever built' and emphasized its immense size (33,000 square feet) and value (at least $200 million). 'I own the top three floors—the whole floor, times three!' He admitted to having once had a neighbor, pointing to a door on the 66th floor. 'I leased that little section to Michael Jackson. I knew him better than anybody.'" *(*Forbes*, 2017)*

"The legendary Barbara Walters interviews Melania Trump and me on a special this Friday night at 10:00 on ABC. Don't miss it!" *(Twitter, 11/19/15)*

THESE ARE SOME OF MY FAVORITE THINGS...
"Many people have commented that my fragrance, 'Success' is the best scent & lasts the longest. Try it & let me know what you think!" *(Twitter, 2/27/13)*

"We're going to have professors and adjunct professors that are absolutely terrific. Terrific people, terrific brains, successful. We are going to have the best of the best." *(Trump University promotional video)*

THESE ARE MY FAVORITE PLACES...
"I own a house in Charlottesville, does anyone know I own a house in Charlottesville? It's in Charlottesville, you'll see. It is the winery. I mean I know a lot about Charlottesville. Charlottesville is a great place that's been very badly hurt over the last couple of days. I own actually one of the largest wineries in the United States. It's in Charlottesville."

"But you also had people that were very fine people on both sides." *(From the infamous "Both sides" speech following Charlottesville protests, 8/15/17. According to Trump Winery's website, "Trump Winery is a registered trade name of Eric Trump Wine Manufacturing LLC, which is not owned, managed or affiliated with Donald J. Trump, The Trump Organization or any of their affiliates.")*

"40 Wall Street actually was the second-tallest building in downtown Manhattan, and it was actually, before the World Trade Center, was the tallest—and then, when they built the World Trade Center, it became known as the second-tallest. And now it's the tallest." *(Comments to local news station WWOR-UPN9, 9/11/01)*

MY FAVORITE COMMERCIAL IS...
(The full script from a Trump Steaks commercial, 2007. Sadly, the product was sold for only two months.)

FIVE THINGS I'M THE BEST AT ARE...
"I build the best buildings, and I'm the biggest developer in New York by far. While that's real estate and this is politics, are they really so different?" *(*The New York Times*, 1999)*

"Sorry losers and haters, but my I.Q. is one of the highest — and you all know it! Please don't feel so stupid or insecure. It's not your fault." *(Twitter, 5/8/13)*

"Part of the beauty of me is that I'm very rich." *(Good Morning America, March 2011)*

"There is nobody who understands the horror of nuclear more than me" *(Rally in Atlanta, Georgia, 6/15/16)*

"...one of the great memories of all time." *(To reporters, after allegedly forgetting name of a widow's Gold Star husband, 10/25/17)*

PEOPLE LOVE ME BECAUSE...
"I could stand in the middle of Fifth Avenue and shoot somebody, and I wouldn't lose any voters, okay? It's, like, incredible." *(Rally in Sioux Center, Iowa, 1/23/16)*

"I have tremendous respect for women and the many roles they serve that are vital to the fabric of our society and our economy." *(Twitter, 3/8/17)*

"No, I wouldn't say I'm a feminist. That would be, maybe, going too far." *(Interview with Piers Morgan, 1/28/18)*

I'M SO POPULAR BECAUSE...
"And by the way, just so you know, I am the least racist person, the least racist person that you've ever seen, the least." *(Rally in Richmond, Virginia, 6/10/16)*

"And did you know my name is in more black songs than any other name in hip-hop? Black entertainers love Donald Trump. Russell Simmons told me that. Russell said, 'You're in more hip-hop songs than any other person,' like five of them lately. That's a great honor for me." *(Playboy, 2004)*

"We had a case where we had an African-American guy who was a fan of mine. Great fan. Great guy! Look at my African-American over here!" *(Rally in Redding, California, 6/3/16)*

MY (FORMER) BEST FRIENDS ARE...
"I want to thank Steve Bannon for his service. He came to the campaign during my run against Crooked Hillary Clinton - it was great! Thanks S" *(Twitter, 8/19/17)*

"Steve Bannon has nothing to do with me or my Presidency. When he was fired, he not only lost his job, he lost his mind." *(Official Statement, 1/3/18)*

"Michael Wolff is a total loser who made up stories in order to sell this really boring and untruthful book. He used Sloppy Steve Bannon, who cried when he got fired and begged for his job. Now Sloppy Steve has been dumped like a dog by almost everyone. Too bad!" *(Twitter, 1/5/18)*

"'Jeff Sessions, a Fitting Selection for Attorney General'" *(Twitter, 11/22/16)*

"I'm very disappointed in Jeff Sessions." *(Interview with* The Wall Street Journal*, 7/25/17)*

SOMEONE I REALLY WANT TO MEET IS...
"I think I'd get along very well with Vladimir Putin. I just think so. People say, 'What do you mean?' I think I would get along well with him." *(Glasgow, Scotland Interview, 7/30/15)*

"Do you think Putin will be going to The Miss Universe Pageant in November in Moscow — if so, will he become my new best friend?" *(Twitter, 6/18/13)*

"I was in Russia, I was in Moscow recently. And I spoke indirectly — and directly — with President Putin, who could not have been nicer." *(Speech at the National Press Club, May 2014)*

"[Putin] called me a genius, I like him so far, I have to tell you." *(Republican Primary Debate, 2/13/16)*

MY FAVORITE FOODS ARE...
"This way you can take the top of the pizza off. You're not just eating the crust. I like not to eat the crust so that we keep the weight down at least as good as possible." *(Response on YouTube after criticism for eating pizza with a knife and fork with Sarah Palin at a Famous Famiglia Pizzaria in Times Square, 2011)*

"The Fish Delight sometimes. The Big Macs are great, the Quarter Pounders with cheese." *(Response to Anderson Cooper asking what he orders at McDonald's, CNN Republican presidential town hall, 2/18/16)*

"I was sitting at the table. We had finished dinner. We're now having dessert. And we had the most beautiful piece of chocolate cake that you've ever seen, and President Xi was enjoying it." *(Interview with Fox Business, 4/12/17)*

(Trump has been photographed eating KFC on his jet during the campaign trail in 2016. According to The Guardian*, he reportedly drinks large amounts of Diet Coke and has swapped Obama's almonds for Lay's potato chips. According to TIME's Donald Trump After Hours, At the dessert course, he gets two scoops of vanilla ice cream with his chocolate cream pie, instead of the single scoop for everyone else.)*

MY FAVORITE QUOTES ARE...
"My favorite part is when Sam has his gun out in the diner and he tells the guy to tell his girlfriend to shut up. Tell that bitch to be cool. Say: 'Bitch be cool.' I love those lines." *(*TrumpNation: The Art of Being The Donald*, 2005)*

"'Be yardstick of quality. Some people aren't used to an environment where excellence is expected.' -- Steve Jobs" *(Twitter, 9/4/12)*

"I've always been a fan of Steve Jobs, especially after watching Apple stock collapse w/out him – but the yacht he built is truly ugly." *(Twitter, 4/23/13)*

"Thank you Kanye, very cool!" *(Edited retweet of Kanye's West's tweet, "You don't have to agree with trump but the mob can't make me not love him. We are both dragon energy. He is my brother. I love everyone. I don't agree with everything anyone does. That's what makes us individuals. And we have the right to independent thought." 4/25/18)*

"You have to learn the rules of the game. And then you have to play better than anyone else. Albert Einstein" *(Twitter, 8/6/2013)*

"It is better to live one day as a lion than 100 years as a sheep." *(Twitter, 2/28/16. Later that day Trump told NBC's* Meet the Press*, "I know who said it. But what difference does it make whether it's Mussolini or somebody else? It's certainly a very interesting quote.")*

ON INAUGURATION DAY, I HAD SO MUCH FUN!
"I'm like, wait a minute. I made a speech. I looked out, the field was, it looked like a million, million and a half people." *(Speech given to the CIA, 1/21/17)*

"I looked over that sea of people, and I said to myself, 'wow', and I've seen crowds before. Big, big crowds. That was some crowd." *(ABC World News Tonight, 1/25/17)*

"Secondly, photographs of the inaugural proceedings were intentionally framed in a way, in one particular tweet, to minimize the enormous support that had gathered on the National Mall. This was the first time in our nation's history that floor coverings have been used to protect the grass on the Mall. That had the effect of highlighting any areas where people were not standing, while in years past the grass eliminated this visual." ***(Statement from former White House Press Secretary Sean Spicer, 1/21/17)***

PEOPLE I LIKE...
"I like Michael Douglas!" ***(Twitter, 5/17/16)***

"Tom is my friend and a total winner!" ***(Twitter, 9/3/15)***

"Tom Brady's a friend of mine. We play golf together—the great quarterback; he's a phenomenal guy, great athlete. I'm with him, and I feel the same age as him." ***(Dr. Oz interview, 9/15/16)***

"Happy Canada Day to all of the great people of Canada and to your Prime Minister and my new found friend @JustinTrudeau. #Canada150" ***(Twitter, 7/1/17)***

"Thank you @BillyJoel- many friends just told me you gave a very kind shoutout at MSG. Appreciate it- love your music!" ***(Twitter, 5/27/16)***

"Happy Cinco de Mayo! The best taco bowls are made in Trump Tower Grill. I love Hispanics!" ***(Twitter, 5/5/16)***

"I like Mexico and love the spirit of Mexican people, but we must protect our borders from people, from all over, pouring into the U.S." ***(Twitter, 6/19/15)***

MORE THINGS I LIKE...
"I like to drive." **(Reuters, *4/27/17)***

"@Amber_Sadler22: Donald Trump and Mitt Romney would be the most dynamic pres/vp combo in history" No, bad chemistry - I like winning!" ***(Twitter, 10/20/14)***

"I've won many club championships. So my life has been about winning. My life has not been about losing." **(TIME *magazine, 2015)***

"You know, I've had great success. Even in golf, I've won many golf club championships. I don't know if you guys play golf. But to win a club championship is hard, literally hard. And you have to beat scratch players. You got a lot of good players." **(TIME *magazine, 2015)***

EVEN MORE THINGS I LIKE...
"You know, it really doesn't matter what they write as long as you've got a young and beautiful piece of ass." **(Esquire, *1991)***

"Oftentimes when I was sleeping with one of the top women in the world I would say to myself, thinking about me as a boy from Queens, 'Can you believe what I am getting?'" **(Think Big: Make it Happen in Business and Life, *2008)***

"I've got to use some Tic Tacs, just in case I start kissing her. You know I'm automatically attracted to beautiful - I just start kissing them." ***(To Billy Bush, 2005)***

THINGS I LIKE ON TV
"This is one of the great inventions of all time—TiVo." ***(TIME's Donald Trump After Hours, 2017)***

"My guilty-pleasure TV show — 'SNL,' starring me. They got great ratings. The best ratings in years. It was a terrific success. I enjoyed doing it. It was 50 percent more than Hillary [Clinton]'s show. That makes me feel good." ***(2015,* People *magazine)***

"Was @foxandfriends just named the most influential show in news? You deserve it - three great people! The many Fake News Hate Shows should study your formula for success!" ***(Twitter, 12/21/17)***

LEADERS I LOOK UP TO
"He's a fantastic guy. ...He took control of Egypt. And he really took control of it." ***(On President Abdel Fattah el-Sisi, Fox Business, 9/22/16)***

"Love your shoes. Boy, those shoes. Man... " ***(To Egyptian President Abdel Fattah el-Sisi at a meeting in Saudi Arabia, 5/21/17)***

"We've had a great relationship." ***(Meeting with Duterte and reporters, 11/13/17)***

"I just wanted to congratulate you because I am hearing of the unbelievable job on the drug problem." ***(Phone call to Duterte, 4/29/17. According to Philippine Senator Antonio Trillanes, more than 20,000 have been killed in Duterte's war on drugs.)***

"He's become a friend of mine. We have a great friendship as countries. I think we're, right now, as close as we have ever been. And a lot of that has to do with the personal relationship." ***(Press conference, 9/21/17)***

"I am a defender of @MileyCyrus, who I think is a good person (and not because she stays at my hotels), but last night's outfit must go!" ***(Twitter, 9/23/13)***

EVEN MORE PEOPLE I LIKE
"I think Eminem is fantastic, and most people think I wouldn't like Eminem." **(Playboy, *2004)***

"The new Pope is a humble man, very much like me, which probably explains why I like him so much!" ***(Twitter, 12/25/13)***

"I don't care what people say, I like Tom Cruise. He works his ass off and never ever quits. He's one of the few true movie stars." ***(Twitter, 7/5/12)***

"Rosie is crude, rude, obnoxious and dumb - other than that I like her very much!" ***(Twitter, 7/11/14)***

"Everyone knows I am right that Robert Pattinson should dump Kristen Stewart. In a couple of years, he will thank me. Be smart, Robert." ***(Twitter, 10/22/12)***

THINGS, PEOPLE AND PLACES I DON'T LIKE
"The 458 People, Places and Things Donald Trump Has Insulted on Twitter: A Complete List," **(The New York Times, *updates ongoing)***

MY PENPAL IS...
"Why would Kim Jong-un insult me by calling me 'old,' when I would NEVER call him 'short and fat?' Oh well, I try so hard to be his friend - and maybe someday that will happen!" ***(Twitter, 11/11/17)***

"North Korean Leader Kim Jong Un just stated that the 'Nuclear Button is on his desk at all times.' Will someone from his depleted and food starved regime please inform him that I too have a Nuclear Button, but it is a much bigger & more powerful one than his, and my Button works!" ***(Twitter, 1/2/18)***

"I told Rex Tillerson, our wonderful Secretary of State, that he is wasting his time trying to negotiate with Little Rocket Man..." ***(Twitter, 10/1/17)***

MY CATCHPHRASE IS...
"The line of 'Make America great again,' the phrase, that was mine, I came up with it about a year ago, and I kept using it, and everybody's using it, they are all loving it. I don't know, I guess I should copyright it, maybe I have copyrighted it." ***(MyFox New York, March 2015)***

WHAT I'VE LEARNED FROM MY MISTAKES...
"I don't think I've made mistakes. Every time somebody said I made a mistake, they do the polls and my numbers go up, so I guess I haven't made any mistakes." **(This Week, *ABC News, 8/16/15)***

"Thank you to Rasmussen for the honest polling. Just hit 50%, which is higher than Cheatin' Obama at the same time in his Administration." ***(Twitter, 4/3/18)***

MY FAVORITE WEATHER IS...
"It's freezing and snowing in New York--we need global warming!" ***(Twitter 11/7/12)***"

"I know much about climate change. I'd be—received environmental awards. And I often joke that this is done for the benefit of China. Obviously, I joke. But this is done for the benefit of China, because China does not do anything to help climate change. They burn everything you could burn; they couldn't care less. They have very—you know, their standards are nothing. But they—in the meantime, they can undercut us on price. So it's very hard on our business." **(Fox & Friends, *1/18/16)***

"You can't use hair spray because hair spray is going to affect the ozone. I'm trying to figure out. Let's see, I'm in my room in New York City and I want to put a little spray so that I can — right? Right? But I hear where they don't want me to use hair spray, they want me to use the pump because the other one which I really like better than going bing, bing, bing — and then it comes out in big globs, right, and you — it's stuck in your hair and you say oh my God, I've got to take a shower again. My hair's all screwed up, right? I want to use hair spray. They say don't use hair spray, it's bad for the ozone. So I'm sitting in this concealed apartment, this concealed unit — you know, I really do live in a very nice apartment, right? But it's sealed, it's beautiful. I don't think anything gets out. And I'm not supposed to be using hair spray." ***(Hilton Head Island, South Carolina, 12/30/15)***

I'M PROUD OF...
"People are proud to be saying Merry Christmas again. I am proud to have led the charge against the assault of our cherished and beautiful phrase. MERRY CHRISTMAS!!!!!" ***(Twitter, 12/24/17)***

"Be sure to watch "The History of WrestleMania" on @ netflix. My interview explains how I supported the event early on. I'm proud of it." ***(Twitter, 2/28/13)***

"People should be proud of the fact that I got Obama to release his birth certificate, which in a recent book he 'miraculously' found." ***(Twitter, 8/22/13)***

"I think Viagra is wonderful if you need it, if you have medical issues, if you've had surgery. I've just never needed it. Frankly, I wouldn't mind if there were an anti-Viagra, something with the opposite effect. I'm not bragging. I'm just lucky. I don't need it." **(Playboy, *2004)***

MY FIVE BEST IDEAS ARE...
"We should have a contest as to which of the Networks, plus CNN and not including Fox, is the most dishonest, corrupt and/or distorted in its political coverage of your favorite President (me). They are all bad. Winner to receive the FAKE NEWS TROPHY!" ***(Twitter, 11/27/17)***

"I had an idea recently. When they send illegals into our country, we charge Mexico $100,000 for every illegal that crosses that border because it's trouble." ***(Sean Hannity's show, July 15, 2015)***

"I never said 'give teachers guns' like was stated on Fake News @CNN & @NBC. What I said was to look at the possibility of giving 'concealed guns to gun adept teachers with military or special training experience - only the best. 20% of teachers, a lot, would now be able to immediately fire back if a savage sicko came to a school with bad intentions. Highly trained teachers would also serve as a deterrent to the cowards that do this. Far more assets at much less cost than guards. A 'gun free' school is a magnet for bad people. ATTACKS WOULD END!" ***(Twitter, 2/22/18)***

"Space is a war-fighting domain, just like the land, air and sea. We may even have a space force." ***(Speech at Miramar Air Station, California, 4/13/18)***

I'M TOUGH BECAUSE...
"I really believe I'd run in there even if I didn't have a weapon." ***(White House, 2/26/18)***

"Crazy Joe Biden is trying to act like a tough guy. Actually, he is weak, both mentally and physically, and yet he threatens me, for the second time, with physical assault. He doesn't know me, but he would go down fast and hard, crying all the way. Don't threaten people Joe!" ***(Twitter, 3/22/18)***

IF I COULD TALK WITH SOMEONE IN THE PAST, IT WOULD BE...
"President Andrew Jackson, who died 16 years before the Civil War started, saw it coming and was angry. Would never have let it happen!" ***(Twitter, 5/1/17)***

I GET THE BEST ADVICE FROM...
"I'm speaking with myself, number one, because I have a very good brain and I've said a lot of things."

"I know what I'm doing and I listen to a lot of people, I talk to a lot of people and at the appropriate time I'll tell you who the people are. But my primary consultant is myself and I have a good instinct for this stuff." ***(MSNBC's* Morning Joe, *3/16/16)***

WHEN I GROW UP, I'M GOING TO BE A GREAT PRESIDENT BECAUSE...
"My entire life, I've watched politicians bragging about how poor they are, how they came from nothing, how poor their parents and grandparents were. And I said to myself, if they can stay so poor for so many generations, maybe this isn't the kind of person we want to be electing to higher office. How smart can they be? They're morons." **(The New York Times, *1999)***

"I will be the greatest jobs president that God ever created." ***(Candidacy announcement, 6/15/2015)***

"I will build a great wall—and nobody builds walls better than me, believe me—and I'll build them very inexpensively. I will build a great, great wall on our southern border, and I will make Mexico pay for that wall. Mark my words." ***(Candidacy announcement, 6/15/2015)***

"I've had a beautiful, I've had a flawless campaign. You'll be writing books about this campaign." ***(ABC News's* This Week, *7/29/16)***

I LOVE WOMEN
"First of all, nobody respects women more than Donald Trump, I'll tell you. Nobody respects women more. My daughter Ivanka always says, 'Daddy, nobody respects women more than you, Daddy, what are they talking about?'" ***(Rally in Eugene, Oregon, 5/6/16)***

"I think the only difference between me and the other candidates is that I'm more honest and my women are more beautiful." **(The New York Times, *1999)***

"I cherish women. I want to help women. I'm going to do things for women that no other candidate will be able to do." ***(CNN's* State of the Union, *8/9/15)***

I KNOW ALL ABOUT...
"I know more about ISIS than the generals do, believe me. I would bomb the shit out of them. I would just bomb those suckers. And, that's right, I'd blow up the pipes. I'd blow up the refineries. I'd blow up every single inch. There would be nothing left." ***(Rally in Fort Dodge, Iowa, 11/12/15)***

"I know our complex tax laws better than anyone who has ever run for president and am the only one who can fix them." ***(Twitter, 10/2/16)***

"The only one to fix the infrastructure of our country is me - roads, airports, bridges. I know how to build, pols only know how to talk!" ***(Twitter, 5/12/15)***

"I am going to save Social Security without any cuts. I know where to get the money from. Nobody else does." ***(Twitter, 5/21/15)***

"I know some of you may think I'm tough and harsh but actually I'm a very compassionate person (with a very high IQ) with strong common sense." ***(Twitter, 4/21/13)***

DOING A GREAT JOB
(A list of Trump's White House associates and lawyers. Those crossed out have been fired or resigned.)

"Everybody wants to work in the White House." ***(White House, 3/6/18)***

WHY I AM THE BEST PRESIDENT
"Here, you can take that, that's the final map of the numbers. It's pretty good, right? The red is obviously us." ***(To reporters, 4/27/17)***

"I was successful, successful, successful. I was always the best athlete, people don't know that. But I was successful at everything I ever did and then I run for president, first time—first time, not three times, not six times. I ran for president first time and lo and behold, I win. And then people say oh, is he a smart person? I'm smarter than all of them put together, but they can't admit it." **(The Wall Street Journal, *1/14/18. In 1999, Trump sought the nomination for the Reform Party.)***

"Just had a very open and successful presidential election. Now professional protesters, incited by the media, are protesting. Very unfair!" ***(Twitter, 11/10/16)***

"I'm a person that wants to tell the truth. I'm an honest person, and what I'm saying, you know is exactly right." ***(Rally in Phoenix, Arizona, 8/22/17)***

"The Paris accord is very unfair at the highest level to the United States." ***(Press conference, 6/2/17)***

"The $20 billion dollar Wall is "peanuts" compared to what Mexico makes from the U.S. NAFTA is a bad joke!" ***(Twitter, 1/1/18)***

"Hillary is too weak to lead on border security-no solutions, no ideas, no credibility.She supported NAFTA, worst deal in US history. #Debate" ***(Twitter, 10/19/16)***

"We look like we're beggars." ***(The Cats Roundtable, 6/28/15)***

"The fact is, this was a horrible, one-sided deal that should have never, ever been made." ***(White House speech, 5/8/18)***

"I make good deals. I don't make bad deals. I make good deals." ***(The Wall Street Journal, 7/25/17)***

"I deal with foreign countries, and despite what you may read, I have unbelievable relationships with all of the foreign leaders. They like me. I like them. You know, it's amazing." ***(The Wall Street Journal, 7/25/17)***

"I don't believe that any president has accomplished as much as this president in the first six or seven months. I really don't believe it." ***(Rally in Phoenix, Arizona, 8/22/17)***

"...Actually, throughout my life, my two greatest assets have been mental stability and being, like, really smart. Crooked Hillary Clinton also played these cards very hard and, as everyone knows, went down in flames. I went from VERY successful businessman, to top T.V. Star.....to President of the United States (on my first try). I think that would qualify as not smart, but genius....and a very stable genius at that!" ***(Twitter, 1/6/18)***

"I know some of you may think I'm tough and harsh but actually I'm a very compassionate person (with a very high IQ) with strong common sense." ***(Twitter, 4/21/13)***

"Time Magazine called to say that I was PROBABLY going to be named 'Man (Person) of the Year,' like last year, but I would have to agree to an interview and a major photo shoot. I said probably is no good and took a pass. Thanks anyway!" ***(Twitter, 11/24/17. Time later denied this interaction.)***

MY FAVORITE TIME COVER
(Though TIME has featured Trump on their cover, the extra laudatory one pictured here is a fake. Trump has it displayed with his golf clubs.)

"My use of social media is not Presidential - it's MODERN DAY PRESIDENTIAL. Make America Great Again!" ***(Twitter, 7/1/17)***

"With the exception of the late, great Abraham Lincoln, I can be more presidential than any president that's ever held this office." ***(Rally in Youngstown, Ohio, 7/25/17)***

"Most people don't even know he was a Republican. Right? Does anyone know? A lot of people don't know that. We have to build that up a little more." ***(Fundraising dinner for House Republicans, 5/21/17)***

"The Gridiron Dinner last night was great fun. I am accomplishing a lot in Washington and have never had a better time doing something, and especially since this is for the American People!" ***(Twitter, 5/4/18)***

"Since taking office I have been very strict on Commercial Aviation. Good news - it was just reported that there were Zero deaths in 2017, the best and safest year on record!" ***(Twitter, 1/2/18)***

"The Stock Market is setting record after record and unemployment is at a 17 year low. So many things accomplished by the Trump Administration, perhaps more than any other President in first year. Sadly, will never be reported correctly by the Fake News Media!" ***(Twitter, 12/23/17)***

"And he referred to my hands if they're small, something else must be small. I guarantee you there's no problem. I guarantee you." ***(Republican Debate, 3/3/16)***

"Of course it is very hard for them to attack me on looks because I'm so good-looking." ***(NBC's* Meet the Press, *8/9/15)***

"Any negative polls are fake news, just like the CNN, ABC, NBC polls in the election." ***(Twitter, 2/6/17)***

Media Lab Books
For inquiries, call 646-838-6637

Copyright 2018 Topix Media Lab

Published by Topix Media Lab
14 Wall Street, Suite 4B
New York, NY 10005

Printed in China

ISBN-13: 978-1-948174-05-3
ISBN-10: 1-948174-05-7

CEO Tony Romando

Vice President and Publisher Phil Sexton
Senior Vice President of Sales and New Markets Tom Mifsud
Vice President of Brand Marketing Joy Bomba
Vice President of Retail Sales & Logistics Linda Greenblatt
Director of Finance Vandana Patel
Manufacturing Director Nancy Puskuldjian
Financial Analyst Matthew Quinn
Brand Marketing Assistant Taylor Hamilton

Editor-in-Chief Jeff Ashworth
Creative Director Steven Charny
Photo Director Dave Weiss
Managing Editor Courtney Kerrigan
Senior Editors Tim Baker, James Ellis

Content Editor Kaytie Norman
Content Designer Michelle Lock
Content Photo Editor Catherine Armanasco
Art Director Susan Dazzo
Assistant Managing Editor Holland Baker
Designer Danielle Santucci
Assistant Editor Alicia Kort
Editorial Assistants Courtney Henderson-Adams, Sean Romano

Co-Founders Bob Lee, Tony Romando